my personal progress helper

CREATED BY DEBORAH OWEN

THE PERSONAL PROGRESS HELPER

THE **BUSIEST GIRLS** USE *personal progress* AS A TOOL TO ACCOMPLISH *WHAT THEY MOST WANT TO DO.* IT BRINGS YOUR *temporal & spiritual* PURSUITS TOGETHER. IT SHOWS YOU THAT WHAT YOU DO ON THE VOLLEYBALL TEAM OR THE CHESS CLUB HAS A **DIRECT RELATIONSHIP WITH WHO YOU ARE AS A** *daughter of God*

JULIE B. BECK

About Me

my name

YW class

favorite scripture

favorite hymn

birthday

YW leaders

favorite school subject

favorite
color

hobbies

friends

talents

when I grow up

YW value

My Personal Progress

TRACKING SHEET

	1	2	3	4	5	6	7	P
F								
DN								
IW								
K								
CA								
GW								
I								
V								

faith

Faith is not to have a *perfect knowledge* of things; therefore if ye have faith ye *hope* for things which are not seen, *which are true.*

Alma 32:21

faith 1

What can I learn about faith from studying the scriptures?

HEBREWS 11

_____
_____
_____
_____
_____

ALMA 32:17-43

_____
_____
_____
_____
_____
_____
_____
_____

faith 1

ETHER 12:6-22

_____
_____
_____
_____
_____
_____
_____
_____
_____
_____

JOSEPH SMITH - HISTORY 1:11-20

_____
_____
_____
_____
_____
_____
_____
_____
_____
_____
_____
_____
_____
_____

faith 1

What can I learn about faith from studying the teachings of living prophets?

list the talks
and articles

Record quotes and impressions
I have while reading

faith 1

Establish a habit of regular personal prayer
in the morning and evening

TRACK AND MEASURE MY PROGRESS OVER

THREE WEEKS

week 1

week 2

week 3

F

faith 1

How has this experience shaped my feelings about faith and prayer?

_____
_____
_____
_____
_____
_____
_____
_____
_____
_____
_____
_____
_____
_____
_____
_____
_____

faith 2

What can I learn about the role of mothers in influencing the faith of their children?

ALMA 56:45-48; 57:21

_____
_____
_____
_____
_____
_____

THE FAMILY: A PROCLAMATION TO THE WORLD

_____
_____
_____
_____
_____
_____
_____
_____

faith 2

what qualities does a woman need to teach children to have faith?

How can these principles help me prepare to be a faithful woman, wife, and mother?

faith 3

What can I learn about living gospel principles with faith?

BIBLE DICTIONARY

_____
_____
_____
_____
_____
_____

TRUE TO THE FAITH

_____
_____
_____
_____
_____
_____
_____
_____
_____

faith 3

My Family Home Evening
Lesson Plan

_____
_____
_____
_____
_____
_____
_____
_____
_____
_____
_____
_____
_____
_____
_____
_____
_____
_____
_____
_____
_____
_____
_____

CHOOSE A GOSPEL PRINCIPLE

RESOURCES
(scriptures, talks, songs, books, pictures, videos)

faith 3

What experiences have strengthened my faith?

_____

_____

_____

_____

_____

_____

_____

_____

_____

_____

_____

_____

_____

_____

_____

_____

_____

_____

_____

_____

_____

_____

faith 4

What insights about the sacrament can I gain from studying the Last Supper?

MATTHEW 26:26-28

_____

_____

_____

_____

_____

MARK 14:22-24

_____

_____

_____

_____

LUKE 22:17-20

_____

_____

_____

_____

faith 4

What thoughts and impressions do I have while pondering the sacrament hymn & prayers?

WEEK ONE

_____
_____
_____
_____
_____

WEEK TWO

_____
_____
_____
_____
_____

WEEK THREE

_____
_____
_____
_____
_____

faith 4

What do I promise as I partake of the sacrament? How can I keep these promises?

_____
_____
_____
_____
_____
_____
_____
_____

How has understanding the sacrament strengthened my faith in Jesus Christ?

_____
_____
_____
_____
_____
_____
_____
_____
_____
_____

faith 5

How can I gain understanding of the Atonement of Jesus Christ?

ISAIAH 53:3-12

_____
_____
_____
_____
_____
_____

JOHN 3:16-17

_____
_____
_____
_____
_____
_____
_____
_____

faith 5

ROMANS 5

_____
_____
_____
_____
_____
_____
_____
_____
_____

2 NEPHI 9:6-7

_____
_____
_____
_____
_____
_____
_____
_____
_____

faith 5

2 NEPHI 9:21-26

_____
_____
_____
_____
_____
_____
_____
_____
_____

ALMA 7:11-13

_____
_____
_____
_____
_____
_____
_____
_____
_____
_____
_____

faith 5

ALMA 34:8-17

_____
_____
_____
_____
_____
_____
_____
_____

DOCTRINE & COVENANTS 19:15-20

_____
_____
_____
_____
_____
_____
_____
_____
_____
_____
_____

faith 5

What has the Savior done for me?

_____
_____
_____
_____
_____
_____
_____
_____
_____
_____
_____
_____
_____
_____
_____
_____
_____
_____
_____
_____
_____
_____
_____

faith 6

How can I increase my understanding of the Plan of Salvation?

1 CORINTHIANS 15:22

_____
_____
_____
_____
_____
_____

REVELATION 12:7-9

_____
_____
_____
_____
_____
_____
_____
_____
_____

faith 6

2 NEPHI 9:1-28

2 NEPHI 11:4-7

DOCTRINE & COVENANTS 76:50-113

_____
_____
_____
_____
_____
_____
_____
_____
_____
_____
_____
_____
_____
_____
_____
_____
_____
_____
_____
_____
_____
_____
_____

faith 6

_____

_____

_____

_____

_____

_____

_____

_____

_____

DOCTRINE & COVENANTS 93:33-34

_____

_____

_____

_____

_____

_____

_____

_____

_____

_____

faith 6

MOSES 4:1-4

_____
_____
_____
_____
_____
_____
_____
_____
_____
_____

ABRAHAM 3:24-27

_____
_____
_____
_____
_____
_____
_____
_____
_____
_____
_____
_____

faith 6

DRAW a picture depicting the Plan of Salvation

faith 6

How does knowledge of the plan affect my actions, help me understand my identity, and strengthen my faith?

faith 7

Why are we commanded to pay tithing?

1 CORINTHIANS 15:22

_____
_____
_____
_____
_____
_____
_____

REVELATION 12:7-9

_____
_____
_____
_____
_____
_____
_____
_____
_____
_____

Obediently pay a full tithe
KEEP TRACK for THREE MONTHS

MONTH ONE

INCREASE	TITHING

MONTH TWO

INCREASE	TITHING

MONTH THREE

INCREASE	TITHING

faith 7

How has paying tithing helped to grow my faith in Heavenly Father?

_____

_____

_____

_____

_____

_____

_____

_____

_____

_____

_____

_____

_____

_____

_____

_____

_____

_____

_____

_____

_____

PERSONALIZED

faith

EXPERIENCE

MY PLAN IS

_____

_____

_____

_____

_____

_____

_____

_____

_____

_____

_____

_____

_____

_____

_____

_____

_____

faith

faith

VALUE PROJECT

BRAINSTORM

What have I learned about faith that I would like to keep studying?

What skills have I gained and would like to continue to develop?

How can I put to action the things I've studied about faith?

What will help me to continue to exercise faith?

_____

_____

_____

_____

_____

_____

_____

_____

_____

_____

_____

faith

VALUE PROJECT

PLAN

my project is...

_____

_____

_____

_____

_____

_____

The steps I will take to execute my project are...

- _____
- _____
- _____
- _____
- _____
- _____
- _____
- _____
- _____
- _____

faith

VALUE PROJECT

EXECUTE

Task Completed	Date	Time

faith

VALUE PROJECT

EVALUATE

How did this project help me apply the value of faith in my life?

_____

_____

_____

_____

_____

_____

_____

_____

_____

_____

_____

_____

_____

_____

_____

_____

_____

_____

faith

TRACKING SHEET

VALUE EXPERIENCE	STARTED	FINISHED
VALUE PROJECT		

divine nature

Be partakers of the *divine nature.* Giving all diligence, add to your faith virtue; and to virtue knowledge; and to knowledge temperance; and to temperance patience; and to patience godliness; and to godliness brotherly kindness; and to brotherly kindness charity.

2 Peter 1:4-7

divine nature 1

What are some divine qualities of a daughter of God?

THE FAMILY: A PROCLAMATION TO THE WORLD

_____

_____

_____

_____

_____

_____

_____

_____

_____

_____

_____

_____

_____

_____

_____

_____

divine nature 1

2 PETER 1

_____
_____
_____
_____
_____
_____

ALMA 7:23-24

_____
_____
_____
_____
_____
_____
_____
_____

DOCTRINE AND COVENANTS 121:45

_____
_____
_____
_____
_____
_____
_____

divine nature 1

How can I develop these divine qualities?

divine nature 2

What can I learn about the eternal divine nature of womanhood & motherhood?

PROVERBS 31:10-31

_____
_____
_____
_____
_____
_____

THE FAMILY: A PROCLAMATION TO THE WORLD

_____
_____
_____
_____
_____
_____
_____
_____
_____

divine nature 2

What can I learn about the eternal divine nature of womanhood & motherhood?

list the talks and articles

Record quotes and impressions I have while reading

_____

_____

_____

_____

_____

_____

_____

_____

_____

_____

_____

_____

_____

_____

_____

_____

_____

_____

A mother I admire is...

What are important attributes for being a mother?

Pick an attribute and strive to develop it for

TWO WEEKS

TRACK AND MEASURE MY PROGRESS

divine nature 3

Who in my family can I work to strengthen my relationship with?

OVER THE COURSE OF

TWO WEEKS

KEEP TRACK OF MY EFFORTS TO SHOW LOVE TO
THEM AND RECORD THEIR DIVINE ATTRIBUTES

date finished

DN

How has this experience helped me to recognize the divine nature in others and the importance of families in God's plan?

_____
_____
_____
_____
_____
_____
_____
_____
_____
_____
_____
_____
_____
_____
_____
_____
_____
_____
_____
_____
_____

divine nature 4

Memorize the Sacrament Prayers
Write them from memory
THE BLESSING ON THE BREAD

_____
_____
_____
_____
_____
_____
_____
_____
_____

THE BLESSING ON THE WATER

_____
_____
_____
_____
_____
_____
_____
_____

divine nature 4

What can I do each day to further develop my divine qualities?

DO SOMETHING TO HELP ME
REMEMBER JESUS CHRIST EVERY DAY FOR

TWO WEEKS

SET GOALS AND RECORD EXPERIENCES EACH DAY

divine nature 4

What experiences have taught me about how keeping covenants helps me to develop divine qualities?

_____
_____
_____
_____
_____
_____
_____
_____
_____
_____
_____
_____
_____
_____
_____
_____
_____
_____
_____
_____

Why is obedience a divine attribute?

LUKE 2:40-51

_____

_____

_____

_____

_____

_____

_____

_____

JOHN 6:38

_____

_____

_____

_____

_____

_____

_____

_____

_____

_____

How can I be more respectful and obedient to my parents?

MAKE A SPECIAL EFFORT TO BE OBEDIENT FOR

TWO WEEKS

TRACK AND RECORD MY PROGRESS

divine nature 5

How have my experiences helped me to understand the divine roles of parents?

_____
_____
_____
_____
_____
_____
_____
_____
_____
_____
_____
_____
_____
_____
_____
_____
_____
_____
_____
_____
_____
_____

divine nature 6

What are some divine qualities?

READ
MATTHEW 5:9
JOHN 15:12
GALATIANS 5:22-23
COLOSSIANS 3:12-17
1 JOHN 4:21
MORONI 7:44-48

List each divine quality
mentioned in my reading

_____
_____
_____
_____
_____

_____
_____
_____
_____
_____
_____
_____
_____
_____
_____
_____
_____

Memorize MY favorite verse

Write it from memory

_____

_____

_____

_____

_____

_____

_____

_____

A divine quality from these verses I need to improve on is...

_____

STRIVE TO DEVELOP THAT QUALITY FOR

TWO WEEKS

TRACK AND RECORD MY PROGRESS

divine nature 6

What experiences have taught me about the importance of developing my divine attributes?

_____
_____
_____
_____
_____
_____
_____
_____
_____
_____
_____
_____
_____
_____
_____
_____
_____
_____
_____
_____

divine nature 7

DEFINITION of PEACEMAKER

_____
_____
_____
_____
_____

find 5 scriptures about peacemakers

What do these scriptures teach about peacemaking?

_____
_____
_____
_____
_____
_____
_____

_____
_____
_____
_____

divine nature 7

How can I be an example through being a peacemaker?

STRIVE TO BECOME A PEACEMAKER FOR

TWO WEEKS

TRACK AND RECORD MY PROGRESS

divine nature 7

How will I continue to develop my divine attributes as I seek to be a peacemaker?

_____

_____

_____

_____

_____

_____

_____

_____

_____

_____

_____

_____

_____

_____

_____

_____

_____

_____

_____

_____

PERSONALIZED

divine nature

EXPERIENCE

MY PLAN IS

_____

_____

_____

_____

_____

_____

_____

_____

_____

_____

_____

_____

_____

_____

_____

_____

divine nature

DN

divine nature

VALUE PROJECT

BRAINSTORM

What have I learned about divine nature that I would like to keep studying?

What skills have I gained and would like to continue to develop?

How can I put to action the things I've studied about my divine nature?

What will help me to continue to understand my divine nature?

_____

_____

_____

_____

_____

_____

_____

_____

_____

_____

_____

_____

_____

divine nature

VALUE PROJECT

PLAN

my project is...

_____
_____
_____
_____
_____
_____
_____

The steps I will take to execute my project are...

- _____
- _____
- _____
- _____
- _____
- _____
- _____
- _____
- _____
- _____
- _____

DN

divine nature

VALUE PROJECT

EXECUTE

Task Completed	Date	Time

DN

divine nature

VALUE PROJECT

EVALUATE

How did this project help me apply the value of divine nature in my life?

D
N

_____

_____

_____

_____

_____

_____

_____

_____

_____

_____

_____

_____

_____

_____

_____

_____

_____

_____

_____

_____

divine nature

TRACKING SHEET

VALUE EXPERIENCE	STARTED	FINISHED
VALUE PROJECT		

individual worth

Remember the *worth of souls* is great in the *sight of God.*

D&C 18:10

IW

individual worth 1

What do these scriptures teach me about
Heavenly Father's love for me?

PSALM 8:4-6

_____

_____

_____

_____

JEREMIAH 1:5

_____

_____

_____

_____

JOHN 13:34

_____

_____

_____

_____

_____

I
W

individual worth 1

DOCTRINE & COVENANTS 18:10

_____

_____

_____

_____

_____

_____

ABRAHAM 3:22-23

_____

_____

_____

_____

_____

_____

_____

_____

JOSEPH SMITH - HISTORY 1:1-20

_____

_____

_____

_____

_____

_____

_____

I
W

Why is it important for me
to know that I am a daughter of God?

I
W

_____
_____
_____
_____
_____
_____
_____
_____
_____
_____
_____
_____
_____
_____
_____
_____
_____
_____
_____
_____
_____
_____

individual worth 2

What is the importance of a patriarchal blessing?

list the talks and articles

Record quotes and impressions I have while reading

I W

individual worth 2

IW

How can I/did I prepare to receive a patriarchal blessing?

_____
_____
_____
_____
_____
_____
_____

How will a patriarchal blessing help me throughout my life?

_____
_____
_____
_____
_____
_____
_____
_____
_____
_____
_____

individual worth 3

Why is it important to help others feel of worth?

DOCTRINE & COVENANTS 18:10

_____
_____
_____
_____
_____
_____

DOCTRINE & COVENANTS 121:45

_____
_____
_____
_____
_____
_____
_____
_____
_____
_____

What can I do to acknowledge the worthwhile qualities in others?

TAKE NOTICE OF OTHERS POSITIVE QUALITIES FOR

TWO WEEKS

TRACK AND RECORD MY EXPERIENCES

individual worth 3

How has my confidence grown as I've worked
to uplift others around me?

I
W

How can I prepare now to fulfill a unique mission on this earth?

DOCTRINE AND COVENANTS 88:119

_____
_____
_____
_____
_____
_____
_____

WHAT ARE MY HOPES & DREAMS?

_____
_____
_____
_____
_____
_____
_____
_____
_____
_____

MY HOME

_____
_____
_____
_____
_____
_____

MY FAMILY

_____
_____
_____
_____
_____
_____

MY EDUCATION

_____
_____
_____
_____
_____
_____
_____

I
W

MY PLAN
TO ACHIEVE MY GOALS

I W

individual worth 5

PARTICIPATE IN A PERFORMANCE

How does developing my talents help me to understand my individual worth?

_____

_____

_____

_____

_____

_____

_____

_____

_____

_____

_____

_____

_____

_____

_____

_____

_____

_____

individual worth 5

How did participating in this performance build by self-confidence?

I W

_____
_____
_____
_____
_____
_____
_____
_____
_____
_____
_____
_____
_____
_____
_____
_____
_____
_____
_____
_____

individual worth 6

What family history information can I learn from living relatives?

_____

_____

_____

_____

_____

_____

_____

_____

_____

_____

_____

_____

_____

_____

_____

_____

_____

_____

IW

My Pedigree Chart

RECORD THE NAMES AND TEMPLE ORDINANCES OF EACH PERSON

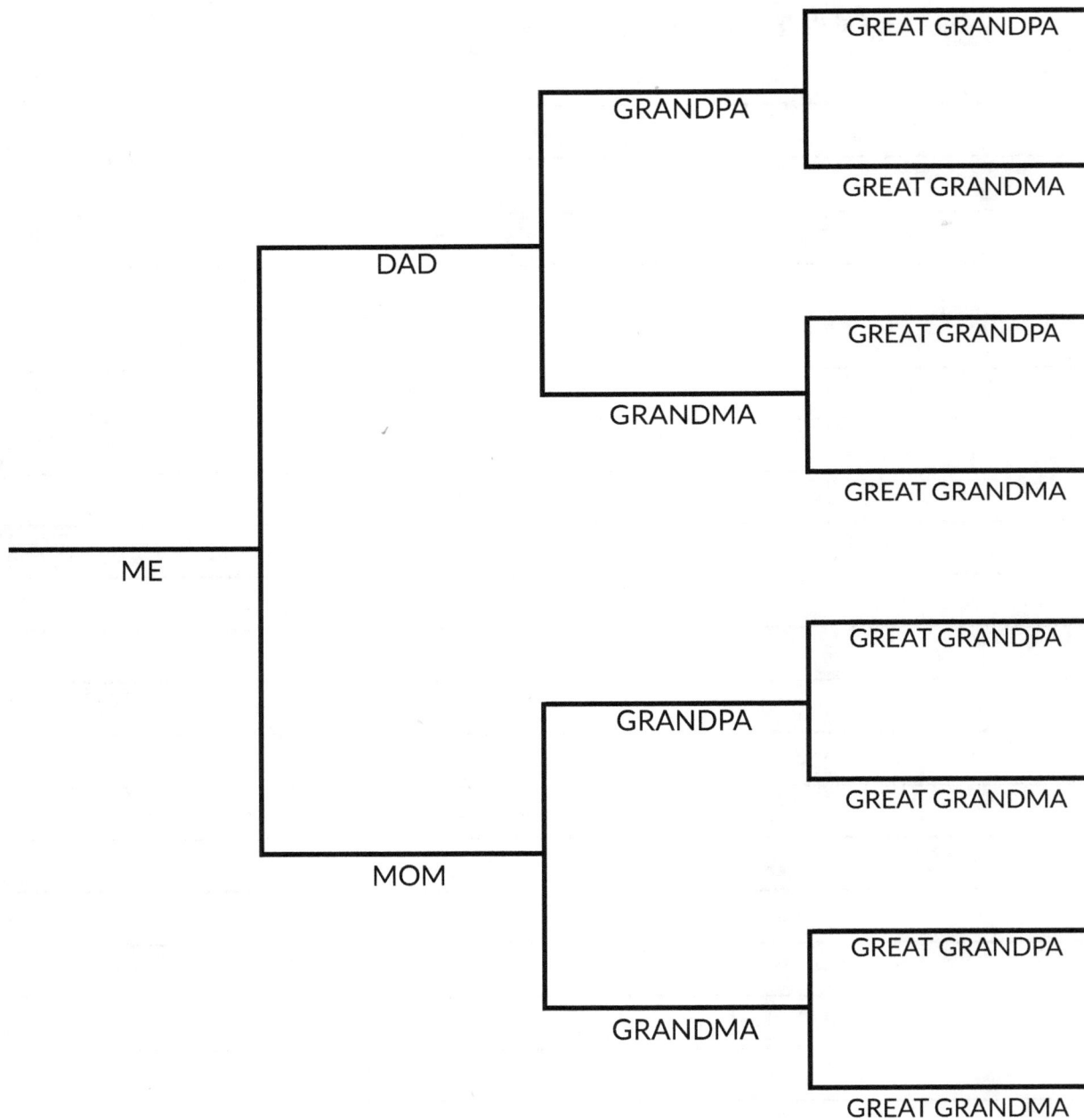

I W

ME

DAD

MOM

GRANDPA

GRANDMA

GRANDPA

GRANDMA

GREAT GRANDPA

GREAT GRANDMA

GREAT GRANDPA

GREAT GRANDMA

GREAT GRANDPA

GREAT GRANDMA

GREAT GRANDPA

GREAT GRANDMA

individual worth 6

How does learning about my heritage teach me about the individual worth of souls?

I
W

individual worth 7

What can I learn about spiritual gifts from Heavenly Father?

1 CORINTHIANS 12:4-12

_____
_____
_____
_____
_____

1 CORINTHIANS 13

_____
_____
_____
_____
_____

MORONI 7:12-13

_____
_____
_____
_____
_____

MORONI 10:8-18

_____

_____

_____

_____

_____

DOCTRINE AND COVENANTS 46:11-26

_____

_____

_____

_____

_____

_____

_____

_____

_____

_____

_____

_____

I
W

individual worth 7

My Divine Qualities

FAMILY MEMBER	YW LEADER	FRIEND

I
W

individual worth 7

How can I continue to develop these gifts and use them to serve others?

_____
_____
_____
_____
_____
_____
_____
_____
_____
_____
_____
_____
_____
_____
_____
_____
_____
_____
_____
_____
_____
_____

I
W

PERSONALIZED

individual worth

EXPERIENCE

IW

MY PLAN IS

_____

_____

_____

_____

_____

_____

_____

_____

_____

_____

_____

_____

_____

_____

_____

_____

_____

individual worth

I
W

individual worth

VALUE PROJECT

BRAINSTORM

What have I learned about individual worth that I would like to keep studying?

What skills have I gained and would like to continue to develop?

How can I put to action the things I've studied about individual worth?

What will help me to continue to understand individual worth?

_____

_____

_____

_____

_____

_____

_____

_____

_____

_____

_____

_____

_____

_____

PLAN

my project is...

_____

_____

_____

_____

_____

_____

_____

The steps I will take to execute my project are...

- _____
- _____
- _____
- _____
- _____
- _____
- _____
- _____
- _____
- _____

I
W

VALUE PROJECT

EXECUTE

Task Completed	Date	Time

VALUE PROJECT

EVALUATE

How did this project help me apply the value of integrity in my life?

_____

_____

_____

_____

_____

_____

_____

_____

_____

_____

_____

_____

_____

_____

_____

_____

_____

I
W

individual worth

TRACKING SHEET

VALUE EXPERIENCE	STARTED	FINISHED
VALUE PROJECT		

IW

knowledge

Seek learning, even by study and also by faith.

D&C 88:118

K

knowledge 1

Why is gaining knowledge as a young woman so important?

PROVERBS 1:5

_____
_____
_____
_____
_____
_____
_____
_____

PROVERBS 4:7

_____
_____
_____
_____
_____
_____
_____
_____
_____

K

knowledge 1

2 NEPHI 28:30

_____

_____

_____

_____

_____

DOCTRINE AND COVENANTS 88:78-80

_____

_____

_____

_____

_____

_____

DOCTRINE AND COVENANTS 88:118

_____

_____

_____

_____

_____

_____

_____

K

knowledge 1

DOCTRINE AND COVENANTS 90:15

_____

_____

_____

_____

_____

DOCTRINE AND COVENANTS 130:18-19

_____

_____

_____

_____

_____

_____

DOCTRINE AND COVENANTS 131:6

_____

_____

_____

_____

_____

_____

K

knowledge 1

How will knowledge of gospel principles bless me and my family?

_____
_____
_____
_____
_____
_____
_____
_____
_____
_____
_____
_____
_____
_____
_____
_____
_____
_____
_____
_____

K

knowledge 2

TALENTS I HAVE

_____
_____
_____
_____
_____
_____
_____
_____
_____
_____
_____
_____
_____
_____
_____
_____

TALENTS I WOULD LIKE TO DEVELOP

_____
_____
_____
_____
_____
_____
_____
_____
_____
_____
_____
_____
_____
_____
_____
_____

knowledge 2

Why is developing talents important?
MATTHEW 25:14-30

_____
_____
_____
_____
_____
_____

What skill or talent will I learn?

_____

What has this experience taught me?

_____
_____
_____
_____
_____
_____
_____
_____
_____
_____
_____

K

knowledge 3

Memorize Article of Faith #13

Write it from memory

_____
_____
_____
_____
_____
_____
_____

Attend a performance or exhibit

_____

Evaluate it using Article of Faith #13 as my guide

HONEST	_____	BELIEVE ALL THINGS	_____
TRUE	_____	HOPE ALL THINGS	_____
CHASTE	_____	ENDURE ALL THINGS	_____
BENEVOLENT	_____	VIRTUOUS	_____
VIRTUOUS	_____	LOVELY	_____
DOING GOOD TO ALL MEN	_____	OF GOOD REPORT	_____
		PRAISEWORTHY	_____

K

knowledge 3

How will making informed decisions help me to keep the companionship of the Holy Ghost?

_____
_____
_____
_____
_____
_____
_____
_____
_____
_____
_____
_____
_____
_____
_____
_____
_____
_____
_____
_____

K

knowledge 4

My Talk
Study Notes

_____
_____
_____
_____
_____
_____
_____
_____
_____
_____
_____
_____
_____
_____
_____
_____
_____
_____
_____

CHOOSE A GOSPEL PRINCIPLE

RESOURCES
(scriptures, talks, articles)

How can I apply this gospel principle in my life?

_____

_____

_____

_____

_____

_____

_____

_____

_____

_____

_____

_____

_____

_____

_____

_____

_____

_____

_____

_____

_____

K

knowledge 5

What area of work am I interested in?

I am talking with _____

What are their responsibilities?

_____
_____
_____
_____

What education did they receive?

_____
_____
_____
_____

What contribution do they make to society?

_____
_____
_____
_____
_____

K

knowledge 5

Why is preparing for a career important for me to do?

_____
_____
_____
_____
_____
_____
_____
_____
_____
_____
_____
_____
_____
_____
_____
_____
_____
_____
_____
_____
_____
_____
_____

K

knowledge 6

Favorite hymn #1:

Draw the correct conducting pattern for this hymn

What does this hymn teach me about the gospel?

_____
_____
_____
_____
_____
_____

_____
_____
_____
_____
_____
_____
_____

OPPORTUNITY TO CONDUCT

_____

Favorite hymn #2:

Draw the correct conducting pattern for this hymn

What does this hymn teach me about the gospel?

_____
_____
_____
_____
_____
_____

K

_____
_____
_____
_____
_____
_____
_____
_____

OPPORTUNITY TO CONDUCT

_____

Why is music an important part of Heavenly Father's plan?

K

knowledge 7

How can I apply the skills I learn at Young Women Camp in my current and future home?

_____

_____

_____

_____

_____

_____

_____

_____

_____

_____

_____

_____

_____

_____

_____

_____

_____

_____

K

EMERGENCY PREPAREDNESS SUPPLIES LIST

K

My Family Home Evening
Lesson Notes

RESOURCES
(scriptures, talks, articles)

K

PERSONALIZED

knowledge

EXPERIENCE

MY PLAN IS

_____
_____
_____
_____
_____
_____
_____
_____
_____
_____
_____
_____
_____
_____
_____
_____
_____
_____
_____
_____
_____

K

knowledge

knowledge

VALUE PROJECT

BRAINSTORM

What have I learned about knowledge that I would like to keep studying?

What skills have I gained and would like to continue to develop?

How can I put to action the things I've studied about knowledge?

What will help me to continue to understand knowledge?

K

knowledge

VALUE PROJECT

PLAN

my project is...

_____
_____
_____
_____
_____
_____
_____

The steps I will take to execute my project are...

- _____
- _____
- _____
- _____
- _____
- _____
- _____
- _____
- _____
- _____

K

VALUE PROJECT

EXECUTE

Task Completed	Date	Time

K

knowledge

VALUE PROJECT

EVALUATE

How did this project help me apply the value of knowledge in my life?

_____

_____

_____

_____

_____

_____

_____

_____

_____

_____

_____

_____

_____

_____

_____

_____

_____

_____

_____

_____

K

knowledge

TRACKING SHEET

VALUE EXPERIENCE	STARTED	FINISHED
VALUE PROJECT		

K

choice and accountability

Choose you this day whom ye will serve; ... but as for me and my house, we will serve the Lord

Joshua 24:15

C
A

choice and accountability 1

Why is it important for me to make wise decisions?

1 NEPHI 15:8

_____
_____
_____
_____
_____

2 NEPHI 32:3

_____
_____
_____
_____
_____

ALMA 34:19-27

_____
_____
_____
_____
_____

C
A

ETHER 2-3

_____
_____
_____
_____
_____
_____
_____
_____
_____
_____
_____
_____
_____
_____
_____
_____

DOCTRINE AND COVENANTS 9:7-9

_____
_____
_____
_____
_____
_____
_____

C
A

Follow a pattern of regular scripture study and prayer
SET A GOAL AND TRACK MY PROGRESS

How does scripture study and prayer help me make wise decisions?

_____

_____

_____

_____

_____

_____

_____

_____

_____

_____

_____

_____

_____

C
A

choice and accountability 2

List each standard in FOR THE STRENGTH OF YOUTH

Why is it important to choose to live righteous standards?

3 STANDARDS
I NEED TO IMRPOVE IN...

1.
2.
3.

Over the course of
THREE WEEKS
Track and record your progress each day

**C
A**

choice and accountability 3

Why is agency such an important gift?

JOSHUA 24:15

_____
_____
_____
_____

2 NEPHI 2

_____
_____
_____
_____

DOCTRINE AND COVENANTS 82:2-10

_____
_____
_____
_____
_____

C
A

How does agency and accountability for consequences help me to progress?

_____
_____
_____
_____
_____
_____
_____
_____
_____
_____
_____
_____
_____
_____
_____
_____
_____
_____
_____

C
A

choice and accountability 4

Why is it important to learn about repentance?

ISAIAH 1:18

_____
_____
_____
_____

ALMA 26:22

_____
_____
_____
_____

ALMA 34:30-35

_____
_____
_____
_____
_____

C
A

MORONI 8:25-26

_____
_____
_____
_____
_____

DOCTRINE AND COVENANTS 19:15-20

_____
_____
_____
_____
_____
_____
_____

DOCTRINE AND COVENANTS 58:42-43

_____
_____
_____
_____
_____
_____
_____

C
A

choice and accountability 4

What does repentance mean to me?

_____

_____

_____

_____

_____

_____

_____

_____

_____

_____

_____

_____

_____

_____

_____

_____

_____

_____

_____

_____

_____

_____

C
A

choice and accountability 5

How can the Holy Ghost help me make correct choices?

EZEKIEL 36:26-27

_____
_____
_____
_____
_____

JOHN 14:26

_____
_____
_____
_____
_____

JOHN 16:13

_____
_____
_____
_____
_____

C
A

GALATIANS 5:22-25

_____
_____
_____
_____
_____
_____
_____
_____

2 NEPHI 32:5

_____
_____
_____
_____
_____
_____
_____
_____
_____
_____
_____

C
A

MORONI 10:4-5

_____
_____
_____
_____
_____
_____
_____
_____

DOCTRINE AND COVENANTS 11:12-14

_____
_____
_____
_____
_____
_____
_____
_____
_____
_____
_____
_____

C
A

How can the Holy Ghost help me each day to make good decisions?

_____

_____

_____

_____

_____

_____

_____

_____

_____

_____

_____

_____

_____

_____

_____

_____

_____

_____

_____

C
A

choice and accountability 6

WHAT DOES THE YOUNG WOMEN THEME TEACH ME ABOUT...

WHO I AM

_____

_____

_____

_____

_____

WHAT I'M SUPPOSED TO DO

_____

_____

_____

_____

_____

WHY I'M SUPPOSED TO DO IT

_____

_____

_____

_____

_____

_____

choice and accountability 6

What will I do each day to be worthy to enter the temple?

C
A

choice and accountability 6

How does making good choices help me to remain free and happy?

C
A

_____
_____
_____
_____
_____
_____
_____
_____
_____
_____
_____
_____
_____
_____
_____
_____
_____
_____
_____
_____

choice and accountability 7

How is making wise decisions a part of Heavenly Father's plan?

MOSES 4:1-4

_____
_____
_____
_____

MOSES 7:32

_____
_____
_____
_____
_____

2 NEPHI 9:51

_____
_____
_____
_____
_____
_____

C
A

FOLLOW A BUDGET FOR *3 MONTHS*

MONTH ONE

INCOME:

TITHING (10%)

SAVINGS

EXPENSES

FOLLOW A BUDGET FOR *3 MONTHS*

MONTH TWO

INCOME:

TITHING (10%)

SAVINGS

EXPENSES

C
A

FOLLOW A BUDGET FOR *3 MONTHS*

MONTH THREE

INCOME:

TITHING (10%)

SAVINGS

EXPENSES

C
A

choice and accountability 7

What have I learned about choice and accountability through keeping a budget?

_____
_____
_____
_____
_____
_____
_____
_____
_____
_____
_____
_____
_____
_____
_____
_____
_____
_____
_____
_____
_____
_____

C
A

PERSONALIZED

choice and accountability

EXPERIENCE

MY PLAN IS

_____

_____

_____

_____

_____

_____

_____

_____

_____

_____

_____

_____

_____

_____

_____

_____

_____

C
A

choice and accountability

C
A

choice and accountability

VALUE PROJECT

BRAINSTORM

What have I learned about choice and accountability that I would like to keep studying?

What skills have I gained and would like to continue to develop?

How can I put to action the things I've studied about choice and accountability?

What will help me to continue to exercise choice and accountability?

_____
_____
_____
_____
_____
_____
_____
_____
_____
_____
_____
_____
_____
_____
_____

choice and accountability

VALUE PROJECT

PLAN

my project is...

_____

_____

_____

_____

_____

_____

_____

The steps I will take to execute my project are...

- _____
- _____
- _____
- _____
- _____
- _____
- _____
- _____
- _____
- _____
- _____

C
A

choice and accountability

VALUE PROJECT

EXECUTE

Task Completed	Date	Time

C
A

choice and accountability

VALUE PROJECT

EVALUATE

How did this project help me apply the value of choice and accountability in my life?

_____

_____

_____

_____

_____

_____

_____

_____

_____

_____

_____

_____

_____

_____

_____

_____

_____

_____

_____

_____

_____

C
A

choice and accountability

TRACKING SHEET

VALUE EXPERIENCE	STARTED	FINISHED
VALUE PROJECT		

good works

Therefore *let your light so shine* before this people, that they may see your *good works* and glorify your Father who is in heaven.

3 Nephi 12:16

G
W

good works 1

Why is service a fundamental principle of the gospel?

MATTHEW 5:13-16

_____

_____

_____

_____

MATTHEW 25:34-40

_____

_____

_____

_____

GALATIANS 6:9-10

_____

_____

_____

_____

_____

G
W

good works 1

JAMES 1:22-27

_____

_____

_____

_____

_____

_____

_____

MOSIAH 2:17

_____

_____

_____

_____

_____

_____

_____

_____

_____

_____

G
W

MOSIAH 4:26

_____

_____

_____

_____

_____

_____

_____

_____

3 NEPHI 13:1-4

_____

_____

_____

_____

_____

_____

_____

_____

_____

G
W

good works 1

RECORD THE QUIET ACTS OF SERVICE YOU OBSERVE FAMILY MEMBERS AND OTHERS PERFORMING FOR

TWO WEEKS

GW

good works 2

WEEKLY MENU

GROCERY LIST

good works 2

WEEKLY MENU

GROCERY LIST

G
W

good works 2

How has serving in the home taught me
about gratitude and humility?

GW

good works 3

How can I help others to bear their burdens?

MOSIAH 18:7-10

_____
_____
_____
_____
_____
_____

1.

2.

3.

G
W

good works 3

How has this experience changed my attitude about service?

_____

_____

_____

_____

_____

_____

_____

_____

_____

_____

_____

_____

_____

_____

_____

_____

_____

_____

_____

_____

_____

GW

good works 4

My Family Home Evening
Lesson Plan about Service

_____

_____

_____

_____

_____

_____

_____

_____

_____

_____

_____

_____

_____

_____

_____

_____

_____

_____

_____

RESOURCES
(scriptures, talks, songs,
books, pictures, videos)

. . . .

. . . .

. . . .

. . . .

. . . .

. . . .

. . . .

. . . .

. . . .

. . . .

. . . .

. . . .

. . . .

. . . .

. . . .

. . . .

GW

good works 5

How can I be anxiously engaged in service in my current and future family?

DOCTRINE AND COVENANTS 58:26-28

_____
_____
_____
_____
_____
_____
_____
_____

The family member who I can help by doing service is...

_____

Some ways I can serve them are...

_____
_____
_____
_____
_____

GW

Develop a pattern of service for at least

ONE MONTH

TRACK AND MEASURE MY PROGRESS

good works 5

How did this experience improve my relationship with my family member?

_____
_____
_____
_____
_____
_____
_____
_____
_____
_____
_____
_____
_____
_____
_____
_____
_____
_____
_____
_____
_____

GW

good works 6

How can I give service outside of my home?

_____

_____

_____

How did this service impact the lives of those whom I served?

_____

_____

_____

_____

_____

_____

_____

_____

_____

_____

_____

_____

_____

_____

G
W

good works 7

Why is it important to be an example?

MATTHEW 24:14

_____
_____
_____
_____
_____

MATTHEW 28:19

_____
_____
_____
_____
_____

DOCTRINE AND COVENANTS 88:81

_____
_____
_____
_____
_____
_____

GW

good works 7

Who could I invite to church?

HOW DID MY EXPERIENCE GO?

G
W

PERSONALIZED

good works

EXPERIENCE

MY PLAN IS

_____

_____

_____

_____

_____

_____

_____

_____

_____

_____

_____

_____

_____

_____

_____

_____

_____

G
W

good works

G
W

good works

VALUE PROJECT

BRAINSTORM

What have I learned about good works that I would like to keep studying?

What skills have I gained and would like to continue to develop?

How can I put to action the things I've studied about good works?

What will help me to continue to implement good works?

_____
_____
_____
_____
_____
_____
_____
_____
_____
_____
_____
_____
_____
_____

GW

PLAN

my project is...

_____

_____

_____

_____

_____

_____

_____

The steps I will take to execute my project are...

- _____
- _____
- _____
- _____
- _____
- _____
- _____
- _____
- _____
- _____

G
W

good works

VALUE PROJECT

EXECUTE

Task Completed	Date	Time

GW

EVALUATE

How did this project help me apply the value of good works in my life?

_____

_____

_____

_____

_____

_____

_____

_____

_____

_____

_____

_____

_____

_____

_____

_____

_____

_____

_____

_____

GW

good works

TRACKING SHEET

VALUE EXPERIENCE	STARTED	FINISHED
VALUE PROJECT		

GW

integrity

Till I die I will
not remove mine
integrity
from me.

Job 27:5

integrity 1

What does it mean to "deny yourselves of all ungodliness"?
MORONI 10:30-33

_____

_____

_____

_____

_____

_____

_____

_____

_____

_____

_____

_____

_____

_____

_____

_____

_____

integrity 1

What does For the Strength of Youth teach about the Lord's standard?

List the STANDARD	List the TEACHING

MY PLAN

to stay morally clean and temple worthy is...

_____

_____

_____

_____

Practice keeping my standards for at least

ONE MONTH

TRACK AND MEASURE MY PROGRESS

integrity 1

What has this experience taught me about the importance of keeping high standards?

_____
_____
_____
_____
_____
_____
_____
_____
_____
_____
_____
_____
_____
_____
_____
_____
_____
_____
_____
_____
_____
_____

integrity 2

DO I AVOID... **NEVER**　　　　　　　　**ALWAYS**

gossip ○ ○ ○ ○ ○ ○ ○

inappropriate jokes ○ ○ ○ ○ ○ ○ ○

swearing & profanity ○ ○ ○ ○ ○ ○ ○

being light-minded about sacred subjects ○ ○ ○ ○ ○ ○ ○

AM I COMPLETELY... **NEVER**　　　　　　　　**ALWAYS**

truthful ○ ○ ○ ○ ○ ○ ○

morally clean ○ ○ ○ ○ ○ ○ ○

honest ○ ○ ○ ○ ○ ○ ○

dependable and trustworthy in schoolwork and other activities ○ ○ ○ ○ ○ ○ ○

integrity 2

How can I improve MY personal integrity?

_____
_____
_____
_____
_____
_____
_____
_____
_____
_____
_____
_____
_____
_____
_____
_____
_____
_____
_____
_____

ONE NEW HABIT

I WANT TO DEVELOP IS...

date finished

integrity 3

how does CHRIST demonstrate integrity?
3 NEPHI 11:10-11

_____
_____
_____
_____
_____

how did JOSEPH demonstrate integrity?
GENESIS 39

_____
_____
_____
_____
_____

how did ESTHER demonstrate integrity?
THE BOOK OF ESTHER

_____
_____
_____
_____
_____

integrity 3

how did JOB demonstrate integrity?
JOB 2:3, 27:3-6

_____
_____
_____
_____
_____
_____

how did SHADRACH, MESHACH, & ABED-NEGO demonstrate integrity?
DANIEL 3

_____
_____
_____
_____
_____
_____

how did DANIEL demonstrate integrity?
DANIEL 6

_____
_____
_____
_____
_____
_____

integrity 3

how did PAUL demonstrate integrity?
ACTS 26

_____
_____
_____
_____
_____

how did HYRUM demonstrate integrity?
D&C 124:15

_____
_____
_____
_____
_____

how did JOSEPH demonstrate integrity?
JOSEPH SMITH - HISTORY 1:21-25

_____
_____
_____
_____
_____
_____

integrity 3

how did I demonstrate integrity?

I

integrity 4

DEFINITION of INTEGRITY

_____
_____
_____

I AM INTERVIEWING... _____

Questions & Answers

_____
_____
_____
_____
_____
_____
_____
_____
_____
_____
_____
_____
_____
_____
_____

How can I make my actions consistent with my knowledge of right and wrong?

_____
_____
_____
_____
_____
_____
_____

What does it mean to ME to have integrity?

_____
_____
_____
_____
_____
_____
_____
_____
_____
_____
_____
_____

integrity 5

How can I personally stand as a witness of God at all times and in all things, and in all places?

_____

_____

_____

_____

_____

_____

_____

_____

_____

_____

_____

_____

_____

_____

CHOOSE A PERSONAL BEHVAIOR TO IMPROVE

integrity 5

Practice improving a personal behavior for
THREE WEEKS
Track and record my progress each day

integrity 6

Practice integrity through fasting on a designated fast Sunday

date finished

What specific purpose will I fast for?

_____
_____

What thoughts and impressions did I have while fasting?

_____
_____
_____
_____
_____
_____
_____
_____
_____
_____

Begin with a prayer   *Close with a prayer*

_____   _____

integrity 7

What issues, trends, and problems weaken the family?

_____
_____
_____
_____
_____
_____
_____
_____
_____
_____
_____
_____
_____
_____
_____
_____

What can I learn about family from...

the First Presidency Message

_____
_____
_____
_____

The Family: A Proclamation to the World

_____
_____
_____
_____
_____

For the Strength of Youth

_____
_____
_____
_____

integrity 7

Research counsel about the family in church magazine articles and talks

list the talks and articles

Record quotes and impressions
I have while reading

_____
_____
_____
_____
_____
_____
_____

_____
_____
_____
_____
_____
_____
_____
_____
_____
_____
_____

What is my plan to strengthen my present family?

_____
_____
_____
_____
_____
_____
_____
_____

What values & traditions will I establish in my future family?

_____
_____
_____
_____
_____
_____
_____
_____
_____
_____

PERSONALIZED

integrity

EXPERIENCE

MY PLAN IS

_____
_____
_____
_____
_____
_____
_____
_____
_____
_____
_____
_____
_____
_____
_____
_____

integrity

integrity

VALUE PROJECT

BRAINSTORM

What have I learned about integrity that I would like to keep studying?

What skills have I gained and would like to continue to develop?

How can I put to action the things I've studied about integrity?

What will help me to continue to exercise integrity?

_____

_____

_____

_____

_____

_____

_____

_____

_____

_____

_____

_____

_____

_____

integrity

VALUE PROJECT

PLAN

my project is...

_____
_____
_____
_____
_____
_____
_____

The steps I will take to execute my project are...

- _____
- _____
- _____
- _____
- _____
- _____
- _____
- _____
- _____
- _____

integrity

VALUE PROJECT

EXECUTE

Task Completed	Date	Time

integrity

VALUE PROJECT

EVALUATE

How did this project help me apply the value of integrity in my life?

_____

_____

_____

_____

_____

_____

_____

_____

_____

_____

_____

_____

_____

_____

_____

_____

_____

_____

_____

_____

integrity

TRACKING SHEET

VALUE EXPERIENCE	STARTED	FINISHED
VALUE PROJECT		

virtue

Who can find a *virtuous woman?* for her price is far above rubies.

Proverbs 31:10

v

virtue 1

Study the meaning and importance of chastity & virtue

MORONI 9:9

_____
_____
_____
_____
_____

JACOB 2:28

_____
_____
_____
_____

THE FAMILY: A PROCLAMATION TO THE WORLD

_____
_____
_____
_____
_____

V

virtue 1

FOR THE STRENGTH OF YOUTH: SEXUAL PURITY

_____

_____

_____

_____

_____

ARTICLE OF FAITH #13

_____

_____

_____

_____

_____

_____

PROVERBS 31:10-31

_____

_____

_____

_____

_____

_____

V

What are the promised blessings of being sexually clean & pure?

_____

_____

_____

_____

_____

_____

_____

How will I commit to be chaste?

_____

_____

_____

_____

_____

_____

_____

_____

V

virtue 2

What are the promised blessings of being worthy of the Holy Ghost?

READ
JOHN 14:26–27
JOHN 15:26
2 NEPHI 32:1–5
D&C 45:57–59
D&C 88:3–4
D&C 121:45–46

_____
_____
_____
_____
_____
_____
_____

_____
_____
_____
_____
_____
_____
_____
_____
_____
_____
_____
_____
_____

virtue 2

When have I felt the guidance of the Holy Ghost in my life?

_____

_____

_____

_____

_____

_____

_____

_____

_____

_____

_____

_____

_____

_____

_____

_____

_____

_____

_____

_____

V

virtue 3

List each question from ALMA 5

Answer each question

_____ _____
_____ _____
_____ _____
_____ _____
_____ _____
_____ _____
_____ _____
_____ _____
_____ _____
_____ _____
_____ _____
_____ _____
_____ _____
_____ _____
_____ _____
_____ _____
_____ _____
_____ _____
_____ _____

V

virtue 3

List each question from ALMA 5

_____
_____
_____
_____
_____
_____
_____
_____
_____
_____
_____
_____
_____
_____
_____
_____
_____
_____
_____
_____
_____
_____
_____
_____

Answer each question

_____
_____
_____
_____
_____
_____
_____
_____
_____
_____
_____
_____
_____
_____
_____
_____
_____
_____
_____
_____
_____
_____
_____
_____

virtue 3

What will I do to remain pure and worthy of the blessings prepared for me in the temple?

_____
_____
_____
_____
_____
_____
_____
_____
_____
_____
_____
_____
_____
_____
_____
_____
_____
_____
_____
_____

V

virtue 4

How does the Atonement enable repentance?

MORONI 10:32-33

_____
_____
_____
_____
_____
_____

THE BOOK OF ENOS

_____
_____
_____
_____
_____

FOR THE STRENGTH OF YOUTH: REPENTANCE

_____
_____
_____
_____
_____

virtue 4

How can I prepare to worthily partake of the sacrament EACH WEEK?

READ THE SACRAMENT PRAYERS

D&C 20:77, 79

_____
_____
_____
_____
_____
_____
_____
_____
_____

What can I do EACH DAY to remain pure and worthy?

_____
_____
_____
_____
_____
_____
_____

V

virtue

VALUE PROJECT

Read The Book of Mormon

1 Nephi ⚪ ⚪ ⚪ ⚪ ⚪ ⚪ ⚪ ⚪ ⚪ ⚪ ⚪ ⚪

⚪ ⚪ ⚪ ⚪ ⚪ ⚪ ⚪ ⚪ 2 Nephi ⚪ ⚪ ⚪

⚪ ⚪ ⚪ ⚪ ⚪ ⚪ ⚪ ⚪ ⚪ ⚪ ⚪ ⚪ ⚪

⚪ ⚪ ⚪ ⚪ ⚪ ⚪ ⚪ ⚪ ⚪ ⚪ ⚪ ⚪ Jacob

⚪ ⚪ ⚪ ⚪ ⚪ ⚪ Enos ⚪ Jarom ⚪ Omni ⚪ Words of

Mormon ⚪ Mosiah ⚪ ⚪ ⚪ ⚪ ⚪ ⚪ ⚪ ⚪

⚪ ⚪ ⚪ ⚪ ⚪ ⚪ ⚪ ⚪ ⚪ ⚪ ⚪ ⚪ ⚪

⚪ ⚪ ⚪ Alma ⚪ ⚪ ⚪ ⚪ ⚪ ⚪ ⚪ ⚪ ⚪

⚪ ⚪ ⚪ ⚪ ⚪ ⚪ ⚪ ⚪ ⚪ ⚪ ⚪ ⚪ ⚪

⚪ ⚪ ⚪ ⚪ ⚪ ⚪ ⚪ ⚪ ⚪ ⚪ ⚪ ⚪ ⚪

⚪ ⚪ ⚪ ⚪ ⚪ ⚪ ⚪ ⚪ ⚪ ⚪ ⚪ ⚪ ⚪

⚪ ⚪ ⚪ ⚪ ⚪ ⚪ ⚪ ⚪ ⚪ ⚪ ⚪ ⚪ ⚪

⚪ ⚪ ⚪ ⚪ ⚪ ⚪ ⚪ Helaman ⚪ ⚪ ⚪ ⚪ ⚪

⚪ ⚪ ⚪ ⚪ ⚪ ⚪ ⚪ ⚪ ⚪ 3 Nephi ⚪ ⚪

⚪ ⚪ ⚪ ⚪ ⚪ ⚪ ⚪ ⚪ ⚪ ⚪ ⚪ ⚪ ⚪

⚪ ⚪ ⚪ ⚪ ⚪ ⚪ ⚪ ⚪ ⚪ ⚪ ⚪ 4 Nephi

⚪ Mormon ⚪ ⚪ ⚪ ⚪ ⚪ ⚪ ⚪ ⚪ Ether ⚪ ⚪

⚪ ⚪ ⚪ ⚪ ⚪ ⚪ ⚪ ⚪ ⚪ ⚪ ⚪ Moroni

⚪ ⚪ ⚪ ⚪ ⚪ ⚪ ⚪ ⚪ Record My Testimony

virtue

VALUE PROJECT

thoughts on 1 Nephi

_____
_____
_____
_____
_____
_____
_____
_____
_____
_____
_____
_____
_____
_____
_____
_____
_____
_____
_____
_____
_____

V

virtue

VALUE PROJECT

thoughts on 2 Nephi

_____

_____

_____

_____

_____

_____

_____

_____

_____

_____

_____

_____

_____

_____

_____

_____

_____

_____

_____

_____

_____

_____

_____

V

virtue

VALUE PROJECT

thoughts on Jacob

_____
_____
_____
_____
_____
_____
_____
_____
_____
_____
_____
_____
_____
_____
_____
_____
_____
_____
_____
_____
_____
_____

virtue

VALUE PROJECT

thoughts on Enos & Jarom

_____
_____
_____
_____
_____
_____
_____
_____
_____
_____
_____
_____
_____
_____
_____
_____
_____
_____
_____
_____

virtue

VALUE PROJECT

thoughts on Omni & Words of Mormon

_____
_____
_____
_____
_____
_____
_____
_____
_____
_____
_____
_____
_____
_____
_____
_____
_____
_____
_____
_____
_____
_____

virtue

VALUE PROJECT

thoughts on Mosiah

_____
_____
_____
_____
_____
_____
_____
_____
_____
_____
_____
_____
_____
_____
_____
_____
_____
_____
_____
_____
_____

virtue

VALUE PROJECT

thoughts on Alma

_____
_____
_____
_____
_____
_____
_____
_____
_____
_____
_____
_____
_____
_____
_____
_____
_____
_____
_____
_____
_____
_____
_____

V

virtue

VALUE PROJECT

thoughts on Alma

_____
_____
_____
_____
_____
_____
_____
_____
_____
_____
_____
_____
_____
_____
_____
_____
_____
_____
_____
_____
_____
_____
_____
_____
_____

virtue

VALUE PROJECT

thoughts on Helaman

_____
_____
_____
_____
_____
_____
_____
_____
_____
_____
_____
_____
_____
_____
_____
_____
_____
_____
_____
_____
_____
_____
_____

V

virtue

VALUE PROJECT

thoughts on 3 Nephi

_____
_____
_____
_____
_____
_____
_____
_____
_____
_____
_____
_____
_____
_____
_____
_____
_____
_____
_____
_____
_____

virtue

VALUE PROJECT

thoughts on 4 Nephi & Mormon

_____
_____
_____
_____
_____
_____
_____
_____
_____
_____
_____
_____
_____
_____
_____
_____
_____
_____
_____
_____
_____
_____

virtue

VALUE PROJECT

thoughts on Ether

_____
_____
_____
_____
_____
_____
_____
_____
_____
_____
_____
_____
_____
_____
_____
_____
_____
_____
_____
_____
_____
_____

virtue

VALUE PROJECT

thoughts on Moroni

_____
_____
_____
_____
_____
_____
_____
_____
_____
_____
_____
_____
_____
_____
_____
_____
_____
_____
_____
_____
_____
_____

virtue

VALUE PROJECT

testimony of the Book of Mormon

_____
_____
_____
_____
_____
_____
_____
_____
_____
_____
_____
_____
_____
_____
_____
_____
_____
_____
_____
_____
_____
_____
_____

VALUE PROJECT

testimony of the Book of Mormon

_____
_____
_____
_____
_____
_____
_____
_____
_____
_____
_____
_____
_____
_____
_____
_____
_____
_____
_____
_____
_____
_____

virtue

TRACKING SHEET

VALUE EXPERIENCE	STARTED	FINISHED
VALUE PROJECT		

Finishing Personal Progress

MEET WITH YOUNG WOMEN LEADER

_____
_____
_____
_____
_____
_____
_____

MEET WITH BISHOP

_____
_____
_____
_____
_____
_____
_____
_____

RECEIVE RECOGNITION

_____
_____
_____
_____
_____
_____
_____

MY TESTIMONY OF PERSONAL PROGRESS

_____
_____
_____
_____
_____
_____
_____
_____
_____
_____
_____
_____
_____
_____
_____
_____
_____
_____
_____
_____
_____

MY TESTIMONY OF PERSONAL PROGRESS

_____
_____
_____
_____
_____
_____
_____
_____
_____
_____
_____
_____
_____
_____
_____
_____
_____
_____
_____
_____
_____
_____
_____
_____

FIND HUNDREDS OF IDEAS FOR PROJECTS, EXPERIENCES, ACTIVITIES, AND MORE ON...

the personal progress helper

Like and follow on Facebook, Pinterest, and Instagram

ThePersonalProgressHelper.com

Facebook.com/PersonalProgressHelper

Pinterest.com/PPHelper

Instagram.com/PersonalProgressHelper

and join the conversation with #PersonalProgressHelper